Relationship Reconnected

Interior and Cover Designer: Michael Cook
Art Producer: Sue Bischofberger
Editor: Carolyn Abate
Production Manager: Oriana Siska
Production Editor: Melissa Edeburn

Illustrations: Satenik_Guzhanina/iStock, cover; photoart985/shutterstock, cover; Fourleaflover/iStock, pp. iv, ix, 18, 36, 61. Author photo: Jordan Thompson

ISBN: Print 978-1-64152-596-1 | eBook 978-1-64152-597-8

Relationship Reconnected

Proven Strategies to
Improve Communication
and Deepen Empathy

David Simonsen, PhD, LMFT

ROCKRIDGE
PRESS

Contents

Introduction

It was at least my 10th time to the home in response to a call about a disturbance related to a fight between a husband and wife. Another police officer and I took the couple into separate rooms and interviewed them. After determining that domestic violence wasn't an issue, we gave them another warning. As we left, I couldn't help but wonder why they didn't just stop arguing.

I responded to many such calls involving arguments between family members. At the time, I didn't much care about the reasons; I just knew it needed to stop. I often kept going to the same locations and interacting with the same people, as I did with this couple. After two years as a police officer, I realized I was merely breaking up fights between people rather than helping them achieve healthier relationships.

To be honest, I didn't know much about how to help people be productive communicators. I simply knew that I wanted to do more. I found numerous online programs that explained the idea of healthy communication and how it was possible to help people change. From that point on, I was all in. I made the decision to become a licensed marriage and family therapist. Fast-forward 20 years, and I have had the honor of helping couples, individuals, and families figure out their life challenges. Much of my work has centered on good communication.

We all want to be connected. We are in relationships to receive and provide love and care. Effectively communicating that we are not getting love and care can be a challenge if we don't have the skills or knowledge to be effective communicators—even with the person we've committed to spend our life with—and ineffective communication is often the cause of heated arguments.

Learning to effectively communicate with the person you care about most deeply can radically improve your relationship. You could start loving and living instead of resenting and regretting. You may be thinking, "Okay, but how?"

That's what this book is all about: the *how*. In my two decades of private practice, I've found that there are two things that help people experience change in their lives. The first is insight: learning about yourself and why you do what you do. The second is tools: getting clear ideas on how to communicate in a way that won't harm your relationship.

This book will show you how to successfully do those two things by teaching you the four steps of an approach called nonviolent communication (NVC). Through this approach, you will learn to listen deeply to others—as well as to yourself—and you will acquire the tools you need to be an effective communicator.

To help you understand the process, I'll use real-life examples of couples I've counseled who faced the same communication challenges you face. (I've changed their names and identifying details to maintain their privacy.) These are people who once thought they were doomed to live a life of disconnection or, even worse, divorce because they couldn't figure out how to communicate better. But through the practice of NVC, they were able to find a way to successfully and happily stay together.

Change is often not easy. If you and your partner make the choice to read this book and practice the skills, you will get to a place where communication becomes easier and more pleasant. You will also learn new things about your partner. And you will learn that becoming a more effective communicator is within your reach.

Note: If domestic violence is an issue in your relationship, please call the National Domestic Violence Hotline at 1-800-799-7233.

PART ONE

Looking Back and Moving Forward

CHAPTER ONE

The Relationship You Have

Welcome, and congratulations for being here. I say this with all sincerity. It may be easy to see that things need to change in your relationship, but the initial step to make the change is usually the hardest one to take. Choosing to read further is a difficult step in a good direction. I have been married for 24 years, and there have been moments when communicating with my spouse was a challenge. Even so, my wife and I didn't give up. Instead, we found a pattern of communication that works for us. I believe that as you move forward in this book, you and your partner will also be able to find a pattern of communication that works for you. Let's begin by exploring where you are and where you want to go, shall we?

HOW DID YOU GET HERE?

It's likely you didn't start out being hurtful and harsh with each other. It's not as if you woke up one morning and your ability to communicate came to a sudden end. Understanding where you came from and how you got where you are is important to get out of the rut you've found yourselves in. You can't really figure out how you arrived at a destination without knowing your starting point, so let's begin there.

In the Beginning

Think for a moment about the time in your life when your only responsibility was to yourself. Maybe it was early in your career or you were still in college, and you had no kids, no car, and no mortgage. You basically did what you wanted to do and when you wanted to do it. You may have had some responsibilities, but they were minimal. Dare I say you were living carefree? Then you met "the one," and they turned your world upside down. The connection between you was nothing short of amazing, and you were willing to meet that other person halfway.

You probably didn't argue much or at all those first few months. As time wore on, sure, you probably started having some arguments, but you got through those disagreements fairly easily. I'm going to go out on a limb and guess that, at this point in your relationship, you were so in love that you never imagined having problems getting along with your partner. The next thing you knew, you were in a committed relationship with long-term plans. Disagreements occurred from time to time, as they naturally would, but you usually argued them out or avoided dealing with the issue.

Relationship Ups and Downs

As time passed and your relationship became more settled, it became less easy to resolve or ignore your disagreements. Why is this? As we all know, initial feelings of intense passion in relationships are common, but so is ignoring red flags around communication. Dr. Helen Fisher, an anthropologist and relationship researcher, reported in the *Journal of Sex Education and Therapy* that falling in love and being high on cocaine involve the same brain chemicals (dopamine and norepinephrine) and activate many of the same brain pathways.

Over time, the cocaine high wears off, and an addict needs to use more and more of the drug to get high. Similarly, the longer you and your partner are together, the more likely it is that the high of the relationship has waned. Without the relationship high, those red flags become obvious and struggles begin. Real life sets in and arguments occur. Be assured that it's completely natural for couples in long-term relationships to have struggles. It's what you do about those struggles that can be the difference between getting a divorce and staying together.

Life Gets in the Way

Your relationship probably started out smoothly, but change is inevitable. You made a long-term commitment with a focus on each other and perhaps on your careers. Fights now revolve around which family to visit over holidays and whose friends to hang out with on the weekends.

If you decided to have children, along comes the first baby, and arguments shift yet again. Who changes the diapers? Who stays home from work when the child gets sick? Who gets up in the middle of the night? Fast-forward a decade or so, and who's chauffeuring the kids to their extracurricular activities? Fast-forward further: Your grandkids are coming for an overnight stay again and you're tired, but your partner is looking forward to the visit.

If you don't have kids, perhaps work travel gets in the way of being able to do things together. Maybe work requires so much time and effort from one or both of you that you don't have time to check in with one another.

The point is that over time, the responsibilities of life get in the way of productive communication between partners. Life becomes less about you as a couple and more about keeping the family machine running. Inequity happens, it doesn't get resolved, and resentments build. Arguments aren't settled, feelings get hurt, and grudges develop.

You may be concerned that if you pause for a moment to see how you're doing in life, you'll feel overwhelmed. Most couples don't take the time to consider the hurt that is happening in their relationship because doing so can be difficult. As a result, they continue to operate on autopilot because it seems easier.

Married Versus Committed

Over the last century, the idea of what a committed relationship is has changed. According to the National Center for Family & Marriage Research (NCFMR), cohabitation has become a typical pathway to family formation in the United States. The number of young and middle-aged Americans who live together has doubled in the past 25 years. Today, 66 percent of married couples lived together prior to their nuptials. In 2013, roughly 5 million children, about 7 percent, were living in families with cohabiting parents. By age 12, some 40 percent of children had spent some time living with parents who were not married but lived together. Whether you are living with your partner, are married to your partner, have kids with your partner, or have no kids with your partner, NVC can work for you. Its goal is simply to help you communicate better with your partner. The information in this book is for all types of people in all types of relationships.

WHEN COMMUNICATION BREAKS DOWN

Many couples don't realize they're in autopilot mode, which can be loosely translated as being in a rut. If this is your experience, it's fair to assume that your communication as a couple is minimal and often not enjoyable. Still, you may go about your days without giving this problem much thought. There are two events, however, that will force you to realize that your relationship is on autopilot: (1) a crisis, such as a teen sneaking out, an emotional affair, or a job loss; and (2) a mental health issue such as depression or anxiety.

If you encounter a crisis and you don't have the skills to resolve it, or if some type of mental health issue is at hand and you can't work your way through it to the other side, your "relationship rut" will become obvious. I've seen it time and again; when faced with serious issues, couples discover that they've lost the ability to effectively communicate with each other. Good communication, however, is key to successful resolution.

During these times, *what* you communicate to your partner is a key indicator of whether a breakup is going to occur. If good communication is key to successful resolution, then destructive communication is just the opposite. Dr. John Gottman is a psychologist who's done research spanning 40 years on divorce prediction and marital stability. In his book *Why Marriages Succeed or Fail*, he states that contempt is a relationship killer. He says, "When contempt begins to overwhelm your relationship you tend to forget entirely your partner's positive qualities, at least while you're feeling upset. You can't remember a single positive quality or act. This immediate decay of admiration is an important reason why contempt ought to be banned from marital interactions."

Contempt is communicated in destructive ways. You, your partner, or both of you may refuse to listen to each other at all. One or both of you may use sarcasm or make hostile jokes about the other. One or both of you may feel so resentful that when one of you does make an attempt to communicate, that attempt is ignored or rebuffed.

Talking But Not Listening

Most couples who've been together for a long time (say, 10 or more years) develop a communication pattern that is similar to a well-worn path. For example, you have a certain way you like the dishes to be set up in the dishwasher, so you decide to be in charge of the dishwashing. There are times when your partner takes over this task. If they don't do it the way you want, you sigh, become passive-aggressive, or just get plain annoyed. Instead of talking it through, you stuff it.

Your partner notices your behavior and asks what's wrong. So you attempt to explain why you are upset and why you like the dishes arranged a certain way, but your partner butts in to defend themselves and their way of doing things. It's a response you've already heard numerous times. You want to be done with it, so you choose either not to listen or to listen only to respond in a way that has nothing to do with what your partner is saying to you. You're listening for inconsistencies or for information to form a rebuttal. When you believe you have enough "ammo," you fire back. You can replace the dishwasher with any other issue in this scenario.

Negative Thought Patterns

It's human nature to focus on the negative. We tend to forget that the person we've been with for years at one point had our best interest in mind. The reality is that they probably still do have our best interest in mind, but the busyness of life and unresolved resentfulness have led us to believe that our partner has it in for us when we argue.

When we get called out on something, it becomes next to impossible to think critically about what was just said. The power of unresolved issues stemming from our childhood experiences with our families and the resentfulness we feel in the current relationship literally stop us from thinking critically. We resort to emotionally driven behaviors, which tend to create negative interactions with our partner. It's this negative interaction that people often get stuck in. The less they are able to work through their negative interactions, the unhappier they become.

Presumptions and Assumptions

When couples get stuck in a particular way of arguing, they tend to make assumptions about each other and fail to listen to the other person's viewpoint. When one partner engages in an argument, the other immediately assumes they are being blamed for something. When this happens, they move into defense mode. They don't listen and simply wait to respond.

People also tend to tell their partners how they are going to act. Then, when what was predicted comes to pass, they point it out and feel superior. This behavior doesn't help resolve issues. Instead, it creates a power struggle. What may have started out as one person wanting to win an argument turns into two people hurting each other and staying stuck in an argument that goes nowhere.

One couple I worked with could never get through an argument. One partner consistently gave up before they could solve anything, feeling there was no point in arguing because they weren't going to come to a resolution anyway. After much conversation, I was able to help this couple see that there was a point to continuing the discussion but in a different and more productive way. Using NVC skills, they stopped making assumptions about how things were going to end up and stayed the course.

Conditional Speaking

When arguments haphazardly come to an end, they tend to do so with an unreasonable or conditional demand. For example, "You need to stop talking like that or don't ever talk to me again." When couples first start arguing, demands are most likely freely met just to get the fight over with. Over time, after numerous unresolved fights and mountains of resentfulness, it becomes more difficult to meet a partner's demands, unreasonable or otherwise. In fact, you may no longer feel the desire to meet any kind of need or want from your partner. This stubbornness fuels more arguments, driving you both into battle again. Fights aren't about simple disagreements over things; they become fights over who is or isn't getting their needs met in the relationship.

Dual Income, No Kids

I have a few couple friends who are DINKs (dual income, no kids). It's fun to joke around with them when they are describing the latest cool (expensive) gadget they bought. I tell them that I buy two of everything because my kids will inevitably break one of them. Although DINKs don't have any children to break their things, they do have communication challenges just like couples with kids. In fact, their communication struggles may be a bit more challenging because DINKs are often focused on their individual interests rather than on something that requires their combined focus, like children. For this reason, they may find it difficult to recognize that they are stuck in a rut. Unless they share an interest, a communication disconnect is highly likely. They need NVC skills just as much as couples with kids do.

A CHANGED REALITY

I'm certain you can remember a time when you and your partner were all about being with each other. You'd get excited to go places together. You'd save seats for each other and even chat on the phone for hours. Back in college, I remember calling my now spouse and talking for at least three hours at a time. You probably had similar experiences. But thinking back to those times, it may seem almost unbelievable that you and your partner ever engaged in that kind of behavior. In fact, maybe now you don't even want to be in the same room with each other. There's no doubt you're still connected, but you've grown distant. You still share a home, but you're roommates more than anything else.

Together but Separate

As you read this, you may be trying to tell yourself that you two still do things together. What are those things? A ballet recital, a Little League game, your boss's house for a barbecue, your in-laws' for Thanksgiving? These outings are probably enjoyable, but they aren't about you as a couple. When was the last time you went out on your own to dinner, a concert, or a movie? As a couple, you should be going out and doing things together, and if you aren't, you are slowly starving your relationship.

I can guess from my experience as a marriage and family therapist that you used to spend meaningful time together. Those moments are what made you decide you were right for each other. Why did that change? Every couple has their own story. Maybe you were going to prove to someone that your love would last. Maybe you worked hard for the relationship in the beginning because you believed in it. Whatever the story, you are still those two people. You've just let other things get in the way.

All Logistics, All the Time

In my house, my wife and I often sit together on Sunday nights and talk through what is going on that week. These check-ins are really important to make sure our household runs smoothly. You may have a similar system in your home where you frequently discuss the details of your everyday life. This type of connection is important, but if it is all you have, you are missing out. Knowing who is taking the dog to the vet or the kid to the dentist speaks to family duty, not connection building. Intimate connection is about making specific time for each other. It's making sure to be purposeful in how you relate to your partner on a personal level.

Disengaged

All these issues together lead to a feeling of disengagement from your relationship, as when you desire connection at the end of a long day, but your spouse wants to zone out with Candy Crush. In the long run, the disengaged individual often begins looking elsewhere for engagement. This search can lead to affairs and divorce. If your attempts to connect are not reciprocated, you will become upset and unmotivated and make fewer and fewer attempts to connect.

There's much you can do to avoid arriving at this place in your relationship, and the journey starts with effective communication. So don't give up. You can still make a change if you and your partner are committed to it. That change will take work, like most things, but it will be worth it. You *can* have your great relationship back.

WHERE DO YOU WANT TO BE?

I see two viable options: You could continue doing what you're doing and remain unhappy, stuck, resentful, and hurt or you could take the knowledge from this book to gain insight into yourself and your relationship and put into practice what you read.

Can you imagine a rekindled relationship? What would it look like? If you used to love being in the outdoors together, maybe it's going hiking with each other to local places. Did you love to travel? Maybe you can plan special three-day weekend getaways again. Perhaps going to concerts and talking about the music all the way home was your thing. This *can* happen again.

My wife and I love to travel in our RV with the family. We do it whenever we get the opportunity. Our kids sometimes complain, but the trips connect us. We know that the complainers will be on their own someday, and we'll have only each other. We plan to continue doing the things we love to do together. You can plan for the same.

Giving and Receiving

A healthy, lasting relationship is about making life better for the other person. However, not everyone understands this truth. Maybe you grew up in a home with parents fighting over who was responsible for tasks and chores. This constant fighting may have taught you to always look out for yourself in a relationship. But relationships aren't just about looking out for yourself. Healthy, long-lasting relationships are filled with giving and receiving. Relationships are not about all things being equal, because in reality, they will never be. Going into a relationship with the idea of giving to make your partner's life better is the ideal.

Cared For and Valued

One of the most common needs of all humans is the need for connection. People do desperate things to get connection, maintain connection, and even end connection. Turn on any reality show; the drama you see is all about connection. On these shows, some are looking for love, while others are looking for help with broken relationships. Some are stuck in a cycle of addiction as a result of dysfunctional connections. Like all of us, they want to be valued and cared for by another. They don't want to be taken for granted. When people feel taken for granted, they start to grow distant in their relationships.

Shared Experiences

When you and your partner have been together for a long time, it's easy to forget that you both need to nurture your relationship. You can do so through shared experiences like watching a TV show, going to a movie, cooking a meal, or taking an overnight trip. Shared experiences give you opportunities to talk to each other about what's going on around you and to reminisce later. These opportunities build a relationship. You can start doing things as a couple again to get your relationship flourishing—and keep it that way.

A NEW WAY TO COMMUNICATE

As mentioned in the introduction, the foundation of this book is rooted in the practice of nonviolent communication. Be aware that this approach has nothing to do with physical violence, even though the term *nonviolent* is used. In this case, it means not harmful to the relationship. If domestic violence is an issue in your relationship, this book is not for you. In fact, you should seek help by calling 1-800-799-7233. With that said, one of the hallmarks of the NVC approach is listening—not just to your partner but also to yourself.

Keep Your Emotions in Check

As a therapist, I hear stories from couples and families about how arguments happen. Hurtful things are said; hurtful actions take place. The common thread in all these stories is that emotions take over, and people do and say things they later regret.

Emotions are driven by events, and feelings are learned behaviors. Allow me to explain what I mean: If you lose a family member, get fired from a job, or experience an act of betrayal, you may feel overwhelmed, frozen, angry, or even shut down. After your initial emotional reaction, you have time to think and process. That's when feelings start. You may have any number of feelings. These feelings reflect how you learned, as a child, to deal with the stuff of life.

If your feelings overwhelm you, you begin to behave emotionally. Think of it this way: You and your partner have an argument, and you become angry (emotion). If you take the time to think about what is really going on, you will discover more than anger. You may feel unloved, unvalued, hurt, or betrayed (feelings). Emotions rise up during a disagreement or argument because people can't make their partner understand what they are feeling deep down and what they need. They get stuck in the emotions of the moment and stop there; feelings don't get examined, and partners get hurt. When people get hurt, they tend to get stuck in a pattern.

Let's be clear: Your feelings are important. But keeping your emotions in check when an issue arises allows you to assess the situation you are in, dig deep, and let your partner know with honesty and openness your deepest needs.

Breaking Old Habits

Arguing with no solution in sight is a habit that you and your partner have fallen into and that you are working to change with this book and NVC. To break this habit, you need to be willing to do things differently and to approach the information you learn here with an open mind. The idea of building the habit of communicating more effectively may seem overwhelming because you know it will require effort and dedication. But remember, replacing any habit with a more useful one requires effort and dedication.

Most important, neither one of you will be perfect at this task, but at least you will be working at it together.

Buy-In from Both Sides

There is always a potential challenge when two people are engaged in a new learning experience. One person may be up for the challenge, and the other may not be as engaged. This communication strategy is one in which both partners must be fully engaged. If only one of you is all in, it won't work. Both of you must be willing to do the hard work.

However, even if it seems that your partner isn't thrilled about trying NVC, don't give up. Chances are your partner would like to reconnect with you as well. So, gather your strength and make the case for this approach. Ask your partner if they think the way you've been communicating with each other is working. Their answer to that question may be all they need to give this approach a try.

Set Up for Success

Once you both start to engage in this new way of communicating and stick to it for a period of time, you will begin to see change. That's not to say there won't be rough patches. It's very easy to slip back into the old, comfortable ways of communicating. Humans are drawn to comfort—it's why we spend so much money on specialty coffee drinks, seek out the warm sun by lounging at the pool, or take walks or hikes. It's no different in relationships. But often in a relationship, the easy and familiar way of communicating isn't the best approach. Making the attempt to learn a new way to communicate can lead to improved intimacy and empathy in your relationship. As I said, it won't always be easy, but the benefits to your relationship will be long lasting.

CHAPTER TWO

The Relationship You Want

What's your definition of a solid, loving relationship? If I had to guess, I'd say it's a relationship where your needs are heard and met by your partner, and vice versa. This might sound too good to be true, but it isn't. Practicing nonviolent communication skills as a couple makes it entirely possible. When applied properly, the techniques enable you to leave behind demands, blame, judgment, and domination to get what you want. Although you will be tempted to continue communicating the way you always have simply because it's what you are familiar with, you will want to keep practicing to enjoy the relationship benefits of effective communication. Learning the NVC approach to communication can improve your relationship and your life.

WHY NVC WORKS

NVC was created by psychologist Marshall Rosenberg in the 1960s. He wanted to find a way to quickly distribute skills that would lead to peace. Since its inception, NVC has been used to broker peace between warring tribes, in prisons, and in schools. It also works well to foster empathy and intimacy in personal relationships, which seem to diminish for many long-term couples.

Let's say the topic of your mother-in-law is a touchy subject in your relationship. You feel she is too involved in your relationship, and your partner disagrees. One couple I worked with consistently struggled around this issue. Their conversations would often end up in loud back-and-forth arguments. Neither was hearing the other. Because they weren't being heard, they would make unreasonable demands of each other: "Go live with your mother then!" one would shout, and the other would respond, "Stop acting like a spoiled brat, or I will!"

When they recognized what was going on for each of them internally by using their NVC skills, they were able to talk about their feelings and needs around the issue. They were able to hear each other on a deep level and make requests of each other that brought them closer to resolving this particular recurring argument.

Currently, when a topic surrounding a touchy issue, like that of a meddling mother-in-law, comes up, you or your partner might become silent or critical because of other possibly unrelated but unresolved issues. Introducing NVC into your relationship requires that you look at those issues in a different way to learn something new. This deeper look makes NVC an effective approach.

The Gap Between Emotions and Words

Have you ever had such a strong emotion about something that you couldn't come up with words to express what you were feeling, or you used words you regretted later? Emotions are usually related to an event. For example, a friend betrays your confidence, or your partner makes a poor financial decision. Events like these create strong emotions, and we often react to strong emotions without thinking. When you are caught in a strong emotion, the thinking part of your brain often gets suspended. Choices made in the midst of emotion can be bad ones, which can negatively affect your relationships.

NVC requires you to be thoughtful about disagreements. Practicing NVC in the midst of an emotional event is ideal, but if you find that you are having a lot of difficulty, you need to take a break to figure out what is going on with your feelings.

TWO-WAY COMMUNICATION

NVC isn't simply about communicating what you need. Yes, that's one part of it, but there are actually two parts. The first component is to be radically honest when expressing a need to your partner, which requires you to dig deep and identify a need. People find this part difficult because they often operate on their emotions, which can change by the hour. A need tends to be constant. For example, a need for connection or a need for companionship doesn't change.

The other component of NVC requires listening to your partner with an empathetic ear. This can be difficult because your own emotions and needs may drown out your ability to hear what your partner is saying and understand what they are feeling. However, when you can be empathetic toward someone, it's a powerful reminder that we are all human.

Focuses on Feelings

NVC focuses on deep feelings rather than on the emotion of the moment. Emotions come and go, but feelings remain constant over time. On Monday, you may dread going into work, but you're fine with it on Friday, for example. It doesn't mean you really dread working there. So rather than focusing on the dread (the emotion), you want to figure out the deep feeling that brings up that dread. Perhaps you feel sad that you don't have more time to yourself.

Is Needs Based

Needs aren't inherently good or bad; they are simply what drive us. We all have similar needs for survival purposes. Take hydration, for example. We feel thirsty and then quench our thirst. Beyond that, what we need to feel fulfilled in our relationships and in life varies from person to person. Most of us haven't learned to sit down and plan how we will fulfill our relationship needs; it's not as simple as drinking that glass of water to satisfy your thirst. However, NVC helps you and your partner identify your needs so those needs can finally be addressed.

Requires Responsibility

In NVC, you are responsible for your feelings and for finding a way to get your needs met. It's not up to your partner to figure it out. Think about that for a moment. If you are each responsible for yourselves and your own feelings, you can stop responding to each other with hostility.

Emphasizes Empathy

NVC emphasizes empathy, the ability to identify and understand the feelings of another. It's important to see your partner as a separate person who has wants, needs, and desires, just as you do. If you each treat your partner as if their only purpose is to meet your needs, you are not even considering things from their perspective. When you can both empathize with each other, you may find that disagreements occur less frequently because you understand each other better.

FIRST, OBSERVE

One of the great things about being human is our ability to discern between good and bad and to explore other issues related to senses, ethics, and morality. This ability stems from our capacity for observing what's going on around us. A key practice in NVC is to simply observe what is happening in your relationship with your partner, without judging it. Here are three ways to accomplish this task.

Observe the Situation

As an old TV detective used to say, "All we want are the facts, ma'am." This is the point of observation. You are focusing on what's observable. In other words, in your communication with your partner, you will be talking about a *specific* instance, not about several other things that may or may not relate to that instance. For example, you may say to your partner, "When you got home today, you went straight into the other room without saying hello." That's an observation. Here's the part that's not: "You do that all the time, and it's really rude and thoughtless. You didn't even consider my feelings. You didn't even have the courtesy to call me today and ask about my appointment." None of that has anything to do with the situation at hand, so keep judgments, assumptions, and other circumstances out of the conversation.

Make Note of the Facts

Mentally observe the facts of a specific situation. Take, for example, dirty dishes in the sink. One partner said they'd do them in a little while, but hours later they aren't done. These are the facts with no meaning attached to them. The NVC-inspired factual statement would be something like "You didn't clean up the dirty dishes when you said you would."

As you begin this process, you might find that there are times when you actually need to write down the facts of a given situation for clarity.

Evaluate Without Emotion

Evaluating a situation without emotion is probably the hardest part of NVC. We often evaluate situations in so many areas of our lives from a place of emotion. In the case of the dirty dishes, although the act of not washing them is more or less benign, couples in long-term relationships may easily see it as something greater than it really is.

They may say something along the lines of "You said you would do the dishes, and once again you haven't done them. I get so tired of always having to remind you to do your part and having to do it myself. You're taking me for granted." Compare that statement with "You didn't clean up the dirty dishes when you said you would." Notice the difference in how the message comes across.

SECOND, IDENTIFY YOUR FEELINGS

During an argument, people generally don't pay attention to what they are really feeling internally because the emotion of the moment is so loud that it gets all the attention. Then they focus on their partner and how their partner "made" them feel. If you've ever said, "You make me angry," you've ignored your internal feelings and blamed your partner for something you need to take responsibility for. In NVC, the goal is to identify your feeling surrounding the argument and not blame your partner for whatever it is that you are feeling.

Tuning In

Getting to what you are actually feeling about what your partner is saying or doing can be tricky. Yet, if you take a second to be mindful in the moment, you could pinpoint a very specific feeling. For example, "I feel scared" is an internal, self-identified feeling. It is very different from "I feel like you are going to leave me," which is a vague, evaluative statement about someone else.

State Your Feeling

When you have the chance to observe the facts and identify how you feel about what you have observed, you can then make an attempt to state your feelings. For example, you'd say, "I feel scared." Although still difficult, it is easier to communicate what you feel if your partner is practicing NVC with you. Tuning in to and stating your feelings doesn't come easy. Remember, you are trying something new.

Use Direct Language

Language around feelings is often imprecise, so the more direct your language, the better. For example, saying something like "This whole situation is making me crazy . . ." is indirect, and your point may not be clearly understood. So, when it comes to expressing your feelings, I encourage you to be direct. Start your statements with "I feel . . ." and then fill in the blank: *hurt, sad, happy,* etc. These are specific feelings that are generally understood by most people.

Exercise: Thinking About Feelings

Take a moment to think about a commonly occurring argument that you and your partner have and the last time you had it. Simply observe it. If you need to, write it down in your notebook, and stick to the facts. When this issue didn't get resolved, what were your feelings around it? Remember, this exercise is only about stating how you felt by using feeling words. You are not evaluating your partner's behavior or judging them for what they said or didn't say. You are simply trying to identify the feelings that were going on inside you.

THIRD, NAME YOUR NEEDS

Needs are common to all people. These needs are not attached to any specific strategy or behavior. They are the things that drive us, that move us. For example, we all need nourishment. We can nourish ourselves in many different ways. The need that isn't met in your relationship isn't about what your partner is or isn't doing for or to you. It's about you and the things that drive you. This is what NVC wants you to name. When you get to a place in your relationship where you say a person is or isn't doing enough of something, you're no longer talking about your needs; it's a judgment against your partner.

What Is Missing Right Now

When you identify your feeling, attach it to a need. So, if you feel lonely, perhaps the thing missing in your relationship (the need that isn't being met) is companionship. Maybe you feel scared and you have a need for security, but you don't feel secure when a particular issue comes up. You must be able to communicate to your partner the need you identify, whatever it is.

Be Honest with Yourself

This process of identifying a feeling and then expressing a need requires real moments of clarity. We might not want to admit it because it makes us feel vulnerable, but we often know deep down what we need. Then, because of pride or protectiveness, we don't let the important people in our lives know that we have a need. For NVC to work, you must overcome this obstacle. Let your partner know you need help being honest about your needs, or keep a journal to honestly express in the moment what you need.

Avoid Victimhood

The process of NVC requires that you take ownership of your feelings and the things that you need in your relationship. If you have a tendency to feel sorry for yourself and view yourself as the victim, you may have difficulty identifying your needs. Do some self-examination. Being a victim generally does not work well in a relationship in which people are trying to start a new way of connecting. One way to self-examine is to take time to be thoughtful about what is going on for you internally.

FOURTH, MAKE THE ASK

Now that you have identified your need, make a request that is connected to it. I know this can be scary. This component of NVC requires some vulnerability, and, for some, that may be a challenge. Maybe you grew up in a home where self-reliance was valued. Maybe in previous relationships you've asked for things, only to be disappointed. This kind of upbringing values protectiveness of self over vulnerability. I encourage you to let go of past experiences and focus on the needs you've identified. Making the ask will be scary; there's no way around it, but once you name it, I promise you it won't seem so overwhelming.

State Your Request

For your identified need to be met, you need to make a request. It should be for the things that will best meet your needs. There are different types of requests based on the need you have in the moment. A request for a solution or a request for connection are two different types of request.

"Would you be willing to spend some time with me this evening?" is a request for connection. A request for a solution might sound like this: "Would you be willing to take the garbage out?"

Keep It Concrete

Many times in relationships, we only hint or drop vague statements about what we want. Sometimes we don't even ask and make assumptions that our partner will just know. When you've identified your need and begin your request, make sure to keep it specific.

Making requests is the goal, but it's often challenging to shift our thinking from making demands (for example, "You need to spend more time with me because I've been feeling lonely") to simply making a request (for example, "Would you be willing to spend an hour with me this evening?").

Avoid Conditions

Demands and conditions are common ways people communicate during disagreements and arguments. We want something, yet instead of making a request, we make a demand and attach a condition. Maybe you feel that your partner doesn't spend enough time with you. You think that demanding more time is the way to sort out your feelings. For example, "Start spending more time with me, or I'm going to start sleeping on the couch." This demanding, conditional way of communicating a need for companionship keeps you from getting the very connection you want from your partner.

BEFORE YOU BEGIN

You've gotten this far, and I want to congratulate you. I know it's been a challenge and you've probably thought about giving up. But you didn't, so kudos to you and your partner. Hopefully you both are ready to dive in!

Ground Rules

Give your full attention. Minimize distractions by setting aside a specific time to practice your communication.

Foster your connection with eye contact. Practice looking each other in the eyes when you are on good terms.

Take steps to reduce anxiety. Deep breathing techniques can help by improving blood flow and getting more oxygen to your brain so you can think more clearly. Breathing also helps you focus on what you feel internally rather than on the emotion you are experiencing in the moment. It's okay to ask for this space while in the middle of an argument.

Exercise patience. I can't emphasize it enough—patience takes practice. Like any new skill, it can't be acquired right away.

Pitfalls

It may seem that NVC is simply about changing your language. If you can just talk differently, then it will work. I believe this is only partially true. Changing how you talk to each other can be helpful. The other big piece of NVC, which is a bit more challenging, is that it's a change in mind-set. If applied correctly, this tool can shift how you think about relationships in general. When you shift your perception of what you're doing, attempts at communication will come much more easily. You will *want* to be empathetic. Once you become empathetic, making requests and listening will be easier.

WHAT WE'VE COVERED

NVC emphasizes sharing your needs. Your actions in your relationship are your attempts to meet those needs; sometimes they are met and sometimes they are unmet. To make a request of your partner, you first have to define your need and then see if they are willing to meet it. If you make demands, you're likely to get stuck in negative communication cycles that go nowhere. Instead of looking at things as "right or wrong," look at things from the perspective of needs.

I will provide specific examples of how NVC works in long-term relationships to create more positive interactions. It puts to rest the old habitual and hurtful cycles that couples often find themselves stuck in. Breaking out of these "ruts" allows you and your partner to rekindle your relationship. Instead of worrying about another unresolved fight, NVC allows you to quickly assess each other's needs and then make requests of each other.

An argument that starts with "Why don't you spend time with me?" can be easily resolved when, through NVC, your partner assesses their need and realizes they are lonely. Instead of demanding, they can make a request. "I need connection. Will you spend time with me?" How much better will your relationship be when these requests can be made easily?

PART TWO

Recreating Connection

CHAPTER THREE

Learning to Observe

The beginning of the NVC process is factually observing what is going on between you and your partner as well as observing what is going on inside of you.

JAMEELA AND MARCUS

Jameela and Marcus have been married for 10 years. They don't have any children. Jameela is from a large, supportive family that has always valued "family time." She told herself that she would always prioritize her family. The "family time" she grew up with usually involved intense communication about a variety of topics. Her family's closeness had created a communication style of easy back-and-forth conversations. This style allowed for passion to bubble right at the surface. Jameela admitted her emotions could be intense at times when she was discussing things.

Marcus had a very different upbringing. He grew up in a home where both parents worked nine-to-five jobs. He also had a younger brother. In his family, communication was not seen as a priority. In fact, it was minimized. Early on, his parents made it very clear that the adults were the ones who did the talking in the house. Children listened. Marcus was led to believe that he, as a child, really had no right to have an opinion. Marcus told me that he often felt shut down by the adults in his life, and that he and his brother weren't really close. When he was excited about something, he simply told a friend or a teacher. He describes his parents as not being bad people. They just didn't have the tools they needed to provide insights into how to communicate well.

During our first few meetings, we started to work on the couple's families of origin. During one session, I noticed extra tension and asked what had happened. Marcus said that he and Jameela had an argument the night before. Jameela had told Marcus her family was getting together the following week, and she wanted him to attend the gathering with her. He sighed and said that was fine. Jameela could tell something was bothering him and asked what was wrong. Marcus indicated that nothing was wrong. Jameela kept asking what was wrong, and Marcus continued to rebuff her questions. Finally, Marcus left the room with Jameela yelling after him.

This pattern of Marcus shutting down and Jameela yelling at him had been going on for years. These arguments were often about different topics, but the result was the same.

WHAT JUST HAPPENED?

On the surface, it seems as if Jameela and Marcus argued about spending time with her family. The real issue is that they have different needs, which led to assumptions and demands. Marcus has a need to connect one-on-one (in this case, with Jameela), and Jameela has a need to connect with many (in this case, her family). Jameela's demand that Marcus better communicate his true feelings wasn't working. Marcus knew that his upbringing had created an inability to communicate clearly with his wife, but he continued to shut down during times when he needed to state his feelings. He felt that his wife's constant prodding to express himself was turning into beratement.

Marcus began making unreasonable demands of Jameela that she forgo the frequent family get-togethers in order to spend time with him. He made assumptions that she'd rather spend time with her family than with him. Jameela assumed Marcus didn't like her family and demanded that he change his attitude toward them. These unreasonable demands led to continued fights between them. Neither was getting their needs met.

When they first got together, Marcus and Jameela had bonded over shared hurt from past relationships, but this bond had slowly dissipated over the years. Now that the hurt was no longer a bonding event for them, their core needs were being exposed. The first step they needed to take in the NVC approach was to observe what was going on between them and within themselves. They needed to stay present, keep judgment out, and be in the moment.

Stay Present

NVC is about staying present in the moment at hand and not generalizing. This means focusing on one event rather than dredging up other arguments or complaining. As we embarked on using the NVC skills, I instructed Jameela and Marcus to think through that recent argument and focus only on what occurred at that time. Marcus could have easily turned to Jameela to complain about how she doesn't want to spend alone time with him, and she could have easily shot back that he never wants to be around her family, but this exchange would derail the process. They needed to stay present with just the facts of the most recent argument so that it could be objectively observed.

No Judgment Allowed

Long-term couples tend to jump to assumptions and judgments when they argue. Jameela and Marcus were no different. Marcus told me that Jameela cares more about her family than him, and Jameela mentioned that she often feels controlled by Marcus. In talking them through this argument, I had to stop them several times because they were making judgments about each other's observations. For example, when Marcus stated the fact that Jameela wanted to go to the family get-together but he didn't, Jameela rolled her eyes and muttered, "That's because he doesn't like being around them; he's jealous of my relationship with them."

Be in the Moment

Because of how our brains work, it was easy for Jameela and Marcus to immediately go back to their old way of arguing. As I mentioned before, think of it as a well-worn path.

The goal of NVC, in this part of the process, is not to take the path that is easy and comfortable; it's to chart new territory. By being present in the moment, you are better able to get your brain to start forging a new path.

It may not always be easy to remain in the moment, but when you start to go off course, it's worth the effort to guide yourself back to the present. Doing so creates an experience of a more effective way of communication. I guided Jameela and Marcus back to the present so that they could continue practicing and get more used to the process.

GET THE FACTS STRAIGHT

Feelings are important, but it's essential to the process to correctly get the facts straight first. Marcus said that Jameela came into the living room and told him about the family get-together. He also added, "I tend to be introverted, and Jameela's family tends to be extroverted." Those were the facts Marcus stated. It would have been easy for Jameela to stick to her assumption that Marcus doesn't like her family, but I instructed the couple to make a leap and trust that, right then, facts were more important than their feelings. Facts are important because they are based in reality and are not subjective.

Take a Mental Snapshot

To start the observation process, it's important to paint a mental picture of the scene. I instructed Jameela and Marcus to think about the room that the argument happened in. I asked questions like "What time of day was it?," "Was the TV on?," and "Did you work that day?" Reconstructing the scene creates a mental document to catalog what occurred. Knowing what was occurring in your environment can provide important clues into what was going on for each partner.

It's About "Who" and "What"

Who was in the room at the time of the argument? Even if it was just the two of you, it's important to get an accurate snapshot. What was the argument about? Was it related to your hobby or work—or family, as it was in Jameela and Marcus's case? Once you've determined the who and the what, take a moment to jot this information down, to practice laying out the facts of the matter. Eventually, this skill will become second nature and you won't need to write the details down. The who and the what are all part of observing the argument without judgment.

Mining for Data

Remember, observation is not about judging or evaluating. It's more like a fact-finding mission—the kind of mission you might undertake when someone has lost something. For example, you might ask, "Where did you last have it?," "Where did you go next?," and so on. You aren't berating the person for being careless; rather, you are helping them put together the pieces of the event to find what's missing. You need to mine for data like this with your partner when you are observing an argument.

STEPPING OUT OF EMOTION

I sometimes crave ice cream, but the type of ice cream varies. One day I want chocolate, and another, I crave Neapolitan. Emotions are similar. One minute I may be angry about something, and an hour later, I'm getting along with the person I just had an argument with. If I had stayed with the anger and fueled it, I would not have been able to effectively communicate with the other person. The following is some advice on how to step out of emotion so you don't hinder the NVC process.

Don't Listen to Your Mind

Has your mind ever played tricks on you—for example, there's a cord on the floor but you're convinced it's a snake? Your mind can also form false impressions while you're in the midst of a disagreement with your partner. As you are trying to work things out, you become convinced that your partner isn't trying as hard as you are or they don't mean what they are saying. Don't listen to your mind. You are trying something different, so stick with it and simply see the "cord" for what it is.

It helps to know that your mind often relies on past experiences to help you navigate current problems. In the case of Jameela, she'd often think Marcus was intentionally trying to push her away, and Marcus often believed Jameela had no interest in getting closer as a couple with some time just for them. Their minds were playing tricks on them, trying to put them back on the old and useless but familiar path of communication. In our work together, I helped the couple recognize this, and they were able to start breaking the pattern that their minds had become accustomed to.

Keep It Neutral

An important part of the NVC process is that you attempt to maintain a neutral, nonjudgmental stance. Remember, stick to just the facts at this point. Like most couples, Jameela and

Marcus were used to their way of arguing, which included judgments, subjective assumptions, and strong emotions. You and your partner are probably no different. Recognize that your mind will be actively working against you as you try to remain neutral because it is used to the way things have been. Continue making the effort to keep it neutral.

Exercise: Observing a Recent Argument

Write down an observational summary of a recent argument you had with your partner. Review the discussion points we've covered so far. Were you able to get the facts straight and keep your emotions out of the conversation? If not, think about what you could have done differently and jot that down. What do you think the most difficult part of the observation process will be for you and your partner? Jameela and Marcus had some initial difficulty because the process felt a bit unnatural, and you may have a similar experience, but it's to be expected at first.

SAMPLE SCRIPT

Jameela asks Marcus to attend a family get-together with her. He responds by saying "fine" and then grumbling a complaint under his breath. Jameela asks him what's wrong, but he won't give her a specific response. After she asks a number of times, she complains that he's acting grumpy. Marcus ends up leaving the room.

Using the first step of NVC in the moment when an argument would normally follow, Jameela needs to make an observation. It's important not to make an assumption for this part of the process to work.

Jameela: "Marcus, when I went into the living room while you were watching TV, I told you about the family get-together and asked you to join me. When I did that, I noticed that something shifted for you and you left the room. Are you feeling uncomfortable with the idea of spending time with my family?"

Notice that Jameela did not say, "You're obviously feeling uncomfortable." That would be an assumption. When she asks the question instead, Marcus can then take a moment to respond yes or no or define more clearly and accurately what he is feeling.

Marcus: "Yes, I feel uncomfortable with the idea of getting together with your family."

Jameela: "Why?"

Marcus: "My family wasn't as close as yours when I was growing up. We didn't have deep conversations. Heck, we barely even fought."

Marcus is making an attempt to describe what his feelings are by describing a factual situation. This situation provides context for the feelings that should be clearly described as well.

Jameela: "So when I talk about spending time with my family, what do you feel?"

Marcus: "Well, I feel jealous. It reminds me of how much I missed out on as a kid with my own family. And I also feel awkward at times because I'm not really comfortable with the openness and loud conversations that happen at those get-togethers."

*Here Marcus is getting to his core feelings. He is not blaming
Jameela for what he is feeling. Instead, he is figuring out what
is going on inside of him and talking about it. The power of
NVC is taking the pressure off and blame from your partner.*

Jameela applied the first principle of NVC—observation—
by starting off with a simple description of the situation and
how Marcus reacted to her request about spending time with
her family. She did not focus on how his reaction made *her*
feel and she did not assume what he was feeling. Instead,
she asked whether he was feeling a certain way. This gave
Marcus the space to answer yes or no, or provide clarity on
what he was feeling with regard to the discussion in question. Her approach made him feel comfortable enough to
open up about what was truly bothering him, and that's a
good beginning.

YOUR OBSERVATION

Did you identify with Jameela and Marcus's scenario? Even
if you've never argued about spending time with extended
family, I'm confident you and your partner have your own
issues that may result in similar arguments. The idea here
is to understand that it is possible to talk through an ongoing
argument. With NVC, the first step is to observe what trans-
pired between you and translate that back to your partner
without making it about *your* emotions.

You can see why it's important for both people in the
relationship to attempt using NVC, rather than just one
of you. You won't get much traction if only one partner is
interested in keeping their emotions out of the conversation. It has to work both ways.

As we move forward, you will have an opportunity to observe your own argument without involving your emotions. If you don't already have notebooks, it's important to get them now to assist you in this process. A number of prompts follow; having something handy to write in will be useful.

PREPARE

As you've been reading, I'm sure some of your issues as a couple have come to mind. It doesn't matter if they're big ("Do we have enough money for our retirement?") or small ("Why is only one person responsible for cleaning the kitchen after dinner?").

Take a moment to reflect on your own unresolved issues. In your notebook, write down at least five unresolved issues that have created some conflict for you as a couple. Choose one of the smaller issues to work through using the first step of NVC. A smaller issue may be easier to work through if there is less emotion to manage and more of an understanding of what the disagreement was really about.

PRACTICE

Now that you've decided on a specific recent argument, in your mind's eye, describe what was going on as this argument began. Who was in the room? What time of day was it? Was the TV on? What was your partner doing? Where were they sitting? If you have kids, were they upstairs or downstairs, inside or outside? Keep mining for data until you have a complete picture.

OBSERVATION EXAMPLE

Once you've logged the details of the argument, it's time to make your observation. Here's an example.

Partner 1: "Last night when I came home from work, you were sitting on the living room couch playing a video game. The kids were upstairs. When I walked through the door, you did not look up from the game, and you didn't say hello. I said hello first, and after that you looked up and then said hello."

Partner 2: "Last night when you came home from work, I was in the middle of a video game. The kids were upstairs doing their homework. When you said hello, I looked up and said hello."

It's okay if your partner's description doesn't match yours; that's the point of this exercise. The goal is to hear the observation of the facts from each of you with no emotions involved. To include emotions would invite judgment and assumptions, and any attempt to resolve the issue would quickly derail.

REFLECTION

You did it! You completed the first step in NVC—making an observation. Take a minute to reflect on what you wrote in your notebook and what you said to each other. How different did it feel to discuss just the facts around the argument rather than involving your emotions? If you were able to do this exercise without emotion and judgment, that's a job well done!

CHAPTER FOUR

Learning to Identify Your Feelings

We all have feelings when we argue, but during a fight, we often don't manage them well or use them wisely. That's about to change. In this chapter, we move from observation to feelings and what's going on internally for each partner in the relationship. This is the second step of NVC: accurately identifying feelings after you have observed the interaction between you and your partner. This skill helps you have a more accurate conversation.

JULIA AND DANIEL

Julia and Daniel have been married for 15 years. They have three school-age children and both work full time. An ongoing frustration in their relationship is the amount of time they spend on activities not related to them as a couple. At issue is Julia's frustration with the time Daniel spends on his trail running, which often takes three to five hours on the weekends.

The couple spends a lot of time driving their children to school and to various activities. The sheer logistics of their lives have forced them at times to put their own needs on hold to meet the needs of their children. Inevitably, they have little to no time to connect with each other. And right now, any time they do squeeze in to spend with each other ends up in a fight. These fights often begin with Daniel telling Julia that he is going to an event with his trail-running club.

At one time in their relationship, Daniel actively encouraged Julia to join him, but after several rejections, he simply stopped asking. When he'd bring it up, they usually got into a fight. Now he keeps his conversations about trail running to a minimum and only brings it up when he's going to an event. Even then, his announcement is usually followed by Julia's criticism that it encroaches on their time as a couple.

Julia and Daniel are at a stalemate. He feels controlled, and she feels that he isn't interested in connecting with her anymore. When he accuses her of being controlling, he sparks an even bigger backlash. The more he accuses her of wanting to control his life, the more upset she becomes and the more she accuses him of not caring about his family.

Julia and Daniel felt isolated from each other with only occasional and limited times of connectedness. When I asked if they still cared for each other, both said they did but that their relationship had lost its spark. Julia said, "We still are kind to each other, but relationships need more than just kindness." Daniel added, "It's important for us to connect, but it's also important for me to run."

This long-time couple was now in a place where any attempt to communicate about nearly anything was met with assumptions and judgments from the other. There was a lot of unresolved hurt floating around between them.

WHAT YOU FEEL

Does Julia and Daniel's situation resonate with you? Do you feel like you and your partner aren't connecting because one of you is participating in an activity instead of spending time as a couple? If this issue isn't relevant to you, think about a recent disagreement you had as a couple. What are the feelings that bubble up to the surface for you when you think about it? When you and your partner experience a communication breakdown, what do you feel? Remember, I'm not talking about the emotions in the moment but the internal feelings you each are experiencing.

Gut Check

In my work with couples, I've found that when it comes to their feelings, people often think one thing but do another. In other words, if someone feels something but doesn't act emotionally, they stay in their brain. Julia and Daniel know in their brains that they care about each other, but their emotions are so strong that they prevent the couple from thinking clearly and effectively.

Pay attention to what your gut is telling you about how you are feeling with regard to the situation, but also to use your brain to acknowledge what your gut is telling you. This is a fine balancing act. When you can get your brain and emotions to work together, NVC will work well.

Physical Cues

Our bodies remind us all the time of what is going on internally. When your heart starts to race, it could mean you are angry or excited about something. When your eyes begin to water, it doesn't necessarily mean that your allergies are acting up. Usually that's a physical indication that

you're talking or thinking about something sad or poignant.
Julia's face would flush as soon as Daniel mentioned trail
running, indicating that she felt sad. Pay attention to your
body's physical cues to get an idea of what you are feeling in
the moment.

IT'S NOT WHAT YOU THINK

We all have an internal monologue that carries on throughout the day. Maybe a coworker dropped the ball on a key
component of a project. But rather than say something, you
internalize your annoyance. Many people do this with their
partners. Remember that argument I asked you to recall?
I'm going to go out on a limb and suggest that you also had
an internal monologue regarding that argument. At some
point, this monologue goes from internal to external. This is
why fights happen.

Julia and Daniel have internal monologues. Julia is
thinking, "I'm mad because Daniel doesn't care about our
family or me. If he did, he wouldn't spend so much time
trail running." Look at that statement for a moment: Julia
is thinking about what she thinks of Daniel's behavior,
not how she feels about his behavior. This is the type of
thought process you need to examine.

Make the Distinction

There is a distinction between what your partner is doing
and what you feel about what they are doing. It's important
to know the difference. Daniel is engaging in a hobby that
takes him away from home. Daniel's hobby does not make
him a bad person. Julia seems to believe that if Daniel
stopped trail running, their relationship would be better, but

it wouldn't. Addressing whether or not Daniel should have a hobby doesn't get to the deeper level of what's at issue in their relationship. Daniel assumes that Julia expects him to just be a husband and father and have no outside interests. Julia believes that Daniel doesn't care about her and therefore engages in this hobby. That's not what she's feeling. What she's feeling is ignored or abandoned, and Daniel is feeling taken for granted.

Dig Deep

Julia and Daniel remain stuck over this ongoing issue because they are making assumptions and judgments about what the other is feeling. As long as they keep doing this, they won't get anywhere. Perhaps you're in a similar situation. You know there is something going on, but you haven't been able to dig deeper. I'll suggest to you and your partner what I suggested to Julia and Daniel: Ask yourselves, "Why am I upset?"

This may seem like a simple question to ask, but the answer can be very profound. When I am in therapy sessions, my clients often ask questions like "Why do I do this?" and "How did I get here?" When they do, I suggest they answer the questions themselves. Often, they know the answer but are too scared to hear it come out. I encourage you to ask yourself questions and to take time to answer them. Digging deep is necessary for this process to work.

The Core Six

We are emotional beings. We each have certain things that evoke emotion within us. One of the things that gets me is military family homecoming videos. I can't *not* watch them, and I know they will make me emotional. When I first explained to Julia and Daniel that strong feelings were at the core of their arguments, they didn't readily buy in to the idea until they explored further. I pointed out that there are six core emotions that can help start the conversation about feelings: happiness, anger, sadness, surprise, fear, and disgust. If you have difficulty defining your feelings, start with the core six and build from there.

USE "I" STATEMENTS

Julia and Daniel fell into a classic cycle of pointing the finger at the other rather than owning their own feelings. We've all done it. It's called shifting blame. Something happens that causes an argument or makes us feel something we'd rather not feel. We immediately say something like "You made me angry (or sad/annoyed/irritated/etc.)." When we speak this way, there's no ownership of what's going on for us.

Julia and Daniel were exceptionally good at this tactic, blaming each other for the feelings they were having. Shifting blame interferes with the ability to communicate effectively. It is much more productive to take ownership and simply state what you feel by using "I" statements. For example, "I feel angry when . . ." Starting off a difficult conversation with this phrase is less threatening because it puts the feelings where they should be: with you.

Take Ownership

When you use an "I" statement, you are taking ownership of your feelings. This isn't something all couples are used to doing. Julia and Daniel certainly weren't. When we spout statements like "You make me so angry when . . ." or "You're always annoying me when . . . ," we are putting responsibility for what we are feeling on the other person. NVC encourages people to look inside themselves to see what is going on. "What am I feeling?" is the question to answer. When your response to that question begins with "I feel . . . ," you are owning your feelings, which can leave your partner feeling much less defensive and also give them space to look inside themselves to see what's going on there, too.

Remove Blame

It's so easy to point the finger at someone else. It's easy because it means we don't really have to look inside ourselves and determine where we may be at fault. Instead of listening to each other, Julia and Daniel would immediately go into attack mode when they detected the slightest hint of blame. Therefore, it's important not to blame your partner when you are having a conversation about an issue you want to resolve. By using "I" statements, you are keeping the blame out of the picture. Think about it: When a child points a finger at another child to get them in trouble, we tell them that it isn't nice, so why would we want to point the finger at our partners?

Exercise: Ask Yourself and Compare

Take out your notebook and jot down your responses to the following questions, going beyond simple yes and no answers:

- Did you recognize some of your own issues as you read Julia and Daniel's example?
- Do you take ownership of your feelings or do you give your partner this responsibility?
- Do you place blame on your partner without considering whether or not you may actually be at fault?
- Do you claim that if your partner would just (fill in the blank), you wouldn't have to (fill in the blank)?
- Where do you think Julia and Daniel went wrong in their efforts at communication?

Compare your answers with your partner's to see where you both stand. Remember, this exercise isn't about judgment; it's about sharing.

SAMPLE SCRIPT

Julia and Daniel care about each other, but you wouldn't know that from listening to them argue. To get to the heart of their ongoing issue and attempt to resolve it, we embarked on the first step of NVC: factual observation regarding their latest fight.

Daniel: "I approached you after dinner to let you know that I want to participate in a running event next Saturday that starts at 6 a.m. and ends at 6 p.m."

Julia: "I was cleaning up the dinner dishes when you told me that you wanted to participate in an all-day event next Saturday."

Once the facts have been established, then comes the work of determining what each partner feels. Identifying feelings in the moment, that is, describing one's inner experience, allows the couple to be vulnerable with each other.

Julia: "I get worried when you are gone all day running because we're married and we're *supposed* to be hanging out together, especially on the weekends."

Daniel sees that Julia is upset; instead of avoiding her and shutting down, he can make an attempt to understand what is going on deeper within her. He needs to make an observation and use empathy to figure out what she may be feeling.

Daniel: "Are you angry because I want to participate in the event?"

By making a guess about her feelings, Daniel gives Julia a chance to look inward and figure out if she's angry or something else. Her initial response is to go to a familiar place.

Julia: "Yes, it seems like you don't want to spend any time with me. I feel rejected by you, because I think couples should do things together."

Daniel is encouraged to stay on task and not let emotion get in the way of figuring out what Julia is feeling about what is being said.

Daniel: "It seems you think my running is an attempt to avoid spending time with you. It must be hard to see me spending time doing my thing when you have such strong feelings about it."

Julia: "Yes, I do have strong feelings, but I want to be respectful of you as well, so it gets hard to talk about it."

As they stay focused on the facts and their individual needs while avoiding the emotion of the moment, the conversation starts to shift toward identifying deeper feelings.

Julia: "I feel disconnected from you when you go running and I haven't seen you all week. I feel scared that we will end up like my parents, in a loveless marriage."

Listening carefully, Daniel begins to feel empathy and responds accordingly.

Daniel: "When you see me making plans to go running, it must be really difficult for you because you're worried it may lead to more and more disconnection between us."

Conversations like these continue to clarify the feelings and, eventually, the needs of each partner.

Once one partner starts to share their needs, the other partner may feel compelled to share something. But starting another conversation about your own unmet needs while discussing your partner's could make your partner feel invalidated.

YOUR FEELINGS

Figuring out what you're feeling in the middle of an argument with your partner is a challenging and difficult task. In the midst of a disagreement, when our emotions get in the way of our ability to empathize, we get stuck judging our partner, attacking them, or making assumptions. We get lost in these thoughts and don't pay attention to our feelings. Learning to identify your feelings without interpretation is a useful skill in all types of relationships—parent-child, workplace, friendships, and so on—but, most important, it can be useful in your relationship with your partner.

PREPARE

In your notebook, write down a recent issue that came up between you and your partner. Put this issue at the top center of your page. As you think about this issue, write down any feelings that come up for you beneath the heading. This exercise isn't about being right; it's about being productive. Were you sad, surprised, disgusted, annoyed, happy? If you have difficulty identifying feeling words, as many people do, search "feeling words" on the Internet. You will find a list to choose from. Aim for 10 to 20 feeling words to describe your feelings surrounding that recent issue.

PRACTICE

Let's get some clarity around these feelings and narrow the list down to three or four to get to those feelings that are at the heart of your issue. Take a moment to think about some other arguments you have had with your partner. Look at the list of feelings you just made and circle any feelings that commonly come up for you in other arguments.

Another way to identify what's at the heart of your issue is to ask yourself, "What feelings does my 13-year-old self have in common with my present-day self?" Be kind to yourself with this one, as it can bring on a flood of emotions.

Circle any feelings on your list that come up for you when you think about your younger self.

A final way to figure out which feelings are at the heart of your issue is to pay attention to what is going on with your body. What are your physical cues? Are you crying? That may indicate sadness or loss. Do you have butterflies in your stomach? That may indicate nervousness or fear. Do you have tension headaches when certain topics come up? That may indicate frustration. Paying attention to these cues from your body can help you identify what you're feeling. Circle any feeling words that stand out for you.

DIALOGUE EXAMPLE

Now that you have these feelings identified, let's connect them with the issue at hand. I will use Julia and Daniel as an example. Julia can now say, "I feel scared when Daniel makes plans to do things without me. I feel worried that our relationship will end up like my parents' relationship."

Use this example and insert your own feelings into your own situation. When you do this, does it give you some hope? How does it feel to be on the verge of starting to communicate in a different way with your partner?

REFLECTION

How do you feel about identifying what you were feeling and writing it down? Was it difficult? Some people grew up in families where talking about feelings was frowned upon and avoided. In cases like this, writing down what you were feeling can be a cathartic experience. Hopefully you found the process useful. If it felt uncomfortable, that's okay, too. Doing uncomfortable things often helps us grow into better people.

CHAPTER FIVE

Acknowledging Your Needs

Figuring out what you need from your partner sounds like a simple task. You've already identified your feelings, so how hard can it be to figure out what you need? It's true that needs are universal; we all have them. But how our needs are best met varies from person to person. Couples often default to getting their needs met by making demands of their partner. But NVC requires a different approach. In this third step of NVC, you're going to focus on how to identify your needs so you can ultimately get what you want from your partner and your relationship—without demanding it.

CHARLIE AND KARI

Charlie and Kari have been married for 20 years. Recently, the last of their children moved out of the house. During their two decades of marriage, Charlie was the primary breadwinner and decision maker, and Kari stayed home with the kids. These roles defined their relationship.

The couple didn't have extreme challenges in their relationship. But with the kids gone, they started to experience some difficulties. They both assumed that with the kids out of the house, they'd be able to pick up where they left off before they had children, but they were starting to realize that wasn't the case.

Charlie still worked throughout the week, so he would look forward to the weekend and often made plans for the two of them without consulting Kari. When he'd talk to her about plans he'd made for them, Kari would usually end up begrudgingly agreeing to do whatever he'd set up. Once they were out, Kari would end up feeling grumpy or irritable, even though Charlie was working hard to make the outings enjoyable for them both.

Negative interactions would begin with Kari saying something snippy to Charlie in response to hearing about the plans he'd made. He would make attempts to help Kari "snap out" of her bad attitude by complimenting her, buying her flowers, rubbing her back, or doing something else he thought might make her feel good. When he'd ask what was bothering her, Kari would say that nothing was wrong. This would go on for a few rounds. Charlie knew something was wrong, but he couldn't figure out what it was. Kari knew something was wrong, but she didn't know how to stop shutting down or snapping at her husband.

When the couple got together with their kids or with friends, they seemed to get along fine and actually enjoyed the time together, but not when it was just the two of them. They were starting to think that maybe they had fallen out of love. When an argument got really bad between them, one or the other would threaten divorce.

At one session, Charlie discussed how he had made plans to go to a work event with Kari, but Kari had responded angrily, accusing him of not considering her feelings or whether she had plans of her own. The argument got out of hand.

YOUR CORE NEEDS

Charlie and Kari met in college on a debate team. They both enjoyed being able to talk through difficult topics. Although they may have not seen eye to eye on some issues, they were certainly able to talk through them to maintain their friendship. Over 20 years of marriage, working, and raising kids, they went astray.

They got distracted from what really mattered to them as a couple and what had attracted them to each other in the first place. They stopped making each other a priority. Getting back in touch with their core needs would strengthen their relationship and help put an end to their arguments.

Remember, needs are what drive us; they are the things that make us tick. In our relationships, we are often unable to identify these core needs because we're just coping with everything that life throws at us—in other words, we're operating on autopilot, as I mentioned earlier.

Human Nature

Charlie and Kari are no different from anyone else. They have needs, just as we all have needs. A core tenet of NVC is that everything we do is an effort to meet those needs.

So when you are feeling angry, upset, glad, or happy, for instance, you have a need that is either being met or unmet. It's just human nature.

However, what might be different is the way in which our needs are met. For example, we all have a need to eat. How we meet this need can be very different for different people. Some people are vegetarians, some are gluten-free, some are on liquid diets—the options are almost endless. This is how it works in relationships. As humans, we all have needs, but how we meet those needs varies.

Life Enriching

Our needs give us purpose. In some cases, our needs keep us alive—our need for hydration, for example. In other cases, our needs, when they are met, enrich our lives, like our needs for companionship, to be respected, to be heard, and to be cared for.

Some of your needs may butt up against your partner's. For example, if you both have a need for control, you may find yourselves in a power struggle. The reverse can also be true: Your need to be physically active may work well with your partner's need to do the same. Knowing what your needs are can help you navigate your relationship much more effectively.

Your Driving Force

Needs motivate us. They push us to accomplish things, but they also prevent us from making things right with people. Needs were the driving force behind Charlie and Kari's fights. Charlie has a need to stay active when he's not at work. Plus, he's been so used to making the decisions in their marriage that making weekend plans seems to fall in line with what he's always done. Kari, meanwhile, feels a need to be included in the planning; she has a need to feel connected as a couple but also to be treated as an equal partner—that is, she has a need for equality. These needs have to be expressed for the repetitive arguments to stop.

LOOK INWARD

Determining what you need can sometimes be difficult. The best way to determine your needs is to look internally at what is going on for you. Your needs are attached to your feelings. Charlie and Kari weren't paying attention to what they were feeling when they argued. They were ignoring their feelings and the needs related to them.

Family Ties

Many people don't realize that when they're having an argument with their partner, it's usually an attempt to address unmet needs that stem back to their childhood. Oftentimes when we disagree with our partners, the issues that most affect us are things we never dealt with as children. For example, if you were controlled as a child and essentially had no voice, as an adult, you may want to make sure that no one controls you; out of this comes your need to be in control.

In the case of Charlie and Kari, both of Charlie's parents worked during the week and stayed home on the weekends. As he got older, Charlie decided very plainly that he didn't want to be sedentary like his parents. Meanwhile, Kari's parents divorced when she was 10 years old, and she spent years being shipped back and forth between her parents' houses with no say. It made her feel powerless. As we talked through their family-of-origin issues, it became clear to Charlie and Kari how their upbringings unknowingly affected their present-day relationship.

Other Relationships

Most of this book focuses on your relationship as a couple, but it's important to recognize that we all have met and unmet needs in a variety of other relationships, including those with our parents, our children, our peers, our friends, our boss, and so on. All of these relationships affect you. In fact, it may even be that unmet needs in your workplace (or elsewhere) spill out into your relationship with your partner.

Although you may have no issues concerning unmet needs when it comes to your partner, it could appear to your partner that you do simply because you are bringing stress and frustration from work into your relationship at home. It's a good idea to ascertain whether this is the case for you throughout this process of looking at your needs.

Gender Roles

Throughout their marriage, Charlie and Kari had fairly specific roles as husband and wife. Charlie would head off to work and provide the financial support the family needed. Kari would stay home and was in charge of kids' appointments, school meetings, and upkeep of the house. They were fine with the specifics of this arrangement while the kids were young. For years, Charlie and Kari took for granted what they were supposed to be doing in the relationship, regardless of what each of them personally needed.

Having specific gender roles may not always cause problems, but it is still important to inwardly observe how these roles affect each of you and determine whether or not needs are being met.

WHAT IS MISSING?

After looking inward and thinking through the situation, Charlie and Kari each determined the need that drove their current argument: Charlie had a need to stay active, and Kari had a need for connection. They each had other needs as well, but these were the needs that were driving their current argument.

Take a moment now for some introspection of your own. Are you able to determine a need that is not being met in your life? It could be a need for safety, a need for connection, a need to be heard by your partner, or any other need. Remember, Charlie and Kari didn't just stumble upon these needs; it took time to identify them.

Time for Truth

It's important to be honest with yourself and determine what drives you. What motivates you in your relationship? What are you fearful of? Determining what you need in your life is a powerful step because you can then stop relying on others to figure it out for you. If you were raised in a family where verbalizing what you need was shot down, you may have learned not to listen to yourself and, in the process, lost your ability to empathize. It's time to move past that.

It is okay to be truthful with yourself and verbalize what you need, and it is okay for others to do so as well. Empathy, both for yourself and others, is called for here. When Charlie and Kari were able to be truthful with themselves about their own needs and able to empathize with the other's needs, they understood each other better.

Feeling Vulnerable

Taking steps to determine what you need can be an uncomfortable process. In therapy sessions, I often encounter people who claim to be independent and able to take care of themselves, but it's usually a clever cover. They've made this statement often enough to block out the reality that they need the companionship of a partner. They may have difficulty identifying this need because it requires some vulnerability and emotional discomfort. However, if they decided to own the need, it could turn their world upside down in a good way. Allowing yourself to feel vulnerable in the process can help you make the improvements you want to see in your relationship.

Call It Out

Once you have determined what you need, actually say it out loud: "I need . . ." This out-loud verbal acknowledgment allows you to start viewing yourself and your relationships differently. If you now know "I need security" and can verbalize this need to yourself, you can also verbalize it to your partner. When you verbalize your need to your partner, they may feel more comfortable verbalizing their needs with you. Charlie and Kari told each other what their needs are, and that started a cycle of understanding each other better.

SAMPLE SCRIPT

After working with Charlie and Kari for a few weeks, we
determined that they each had some unmet needs that were
causing them difficulties in connecting. Charlie was able to
clearly identify his need to be active on the weekends. He
believes this need came from growing up in a sedentary
household. If nothing was planned for the weekend, he
would become anxious.

Kari determined that she had a need for companionship
and equality in the relationship. When she didn't get that,
she would feel rejected and powerless. Companionship for
Kari meant not only having a partner to connect with but
also playing a part in decision making. However, instead
of addressing her need head-on, she would get snippy and
annoyed with Charlie.

I got Kari to express herself after a heated argument
during one of our sessions. Charlie had once again planned
a trip for the two of them, and Kari felt disconnected and out
of the loop.

Kari: "I can't stand it when you plan a trip for us. You don't include me in anything. You map it all out without asking me what I want to do or where I want to go."

Charlie: "I'm just trying to plan some fun for us. Why does that bother you?"

Charlie is indirectly asking Kari about her feelings as well as making an assumption about what is going on inside her. Perhaps it doesn't bother her, maybe she is upset about something else. It could be that she is not feeling well. When we assume things, we often risk being hurtful and judgmental.

Kari: "I feel unsettled because when you make all the plans without consulting me, I don't feel like we're in it together."

Kari makes an attempt to talk about what she feels. She is not identifying her need here. She is close to blaming Charlie for what she feels, which would be unhelpful to both of them.

Charlie: "I was trying to be helpful. You spent years doing everything for everyone else."

Kari: "I appreciate that you recognize that. But now I want to do it myself and with you as well."

Kari is getting closer to identifying her needs here. As I talked with them more, I stressed the importance of going directly to what the need is and not "dancing" around it. You will stay stuck if you aren't courageous and don't describe the need. Kari was finally able to do it.

Charlie: "I get that. I guess I didn't really think about that."

Kari: "Don't get me wrong, I'd still like you to do nice things for me, but I would feel more connected to you if we could plan trips and outings together."

Charlie: "I will include you in the planning."

This awareness of what's going on internally for Kari radically steered the conversation away from blame and shame. It moved her toward a more cooperative style of interaction for future conversations around hard topics.

The exchange was difficult for Kari, but it paid off. Now Charlie includes Kari in planning what they will do because he understands her need to feel connected to the decision-making process. Kari also understands the importance of activity to Charlie. Charlie told me in a later session: "I realized I had taken Kari for granted. With the kids gone I've found a new appreciation for her."

YOUR NEEDS

You may or may not relate to Charlie and Kari's problem, but I hope you see how NVC skills can be useful in your relationship regardless of your particular issues or communication problems. When you identify a need surrounding an argument and you can each voice that need to your partner, you are practicing effective communication.

PREPARE

In your notebook, write down up to five needs that might be related to a topic you frequently argue about. Perhaps it might be one you identified in a previous exercise. Remember, needs are what drive you. If you are driven by connecting with others, perhaps your need for connection is not being met in your relationship. Do you feel rejuvenated when you spend time alone? Is this need for solitude being met? If not, write it down. Maybe your relationship is loud and aggressive, and you need peacefulness in your life. If so, write that down. The idea here is to identify your needs with regard to a particular issue you and your partner are having.

PRACTICE

As I mentioned earlier, empathy is an important part of the process. It's about being sensitive to your feelings and your partner's feelings. If you aren't used to being empathetic, it will take some getting used to. Think about your most recent argument and take time to tune in to the feelings that came up. Which unmet needs do you think are related to those feelings? Take your best guess. Can you figure out where those needs come from? Think about how you will verbalize your needs to your partner.

DIALOGUE EXAMPLE

Now that you have determined your need or needs with regard to your issue, come up with a sentence or two stating what that need is and write it down. Let's use Kari's need as an example and look at how she verbalized it to Charlie.

Kari: "I need to have a voice in our plans; it makes me feel connected and equal in our relationship. Making plans together will fulfill that need."

Charlie: "I hear that you worry about us not being connected and equal in our relationship, and this causes some anxiety in you. It sounds like you need me to be more communicative around making plans together."

You are probably getting the idea that needs and feelings are often interwoven in the same statement. That's to be expected since they are interwoven. Remember, you won't necessarily state your needs this succinctly right away. What's important is that you try to communicate what you need in your relationship—and keep trying.

REFLECTION

How did it feel to write out the statement expressing your needs? Did you read the statement aloud? Did you read it to your partner? If not, do so when you get a chance. Stating your needs can be a very freeing experience. It may also cause some stress. If stating your needs causes stress for you, it might be because it feels strange. Human beings tend to choose comfort over discomfort. However, if we can get past the initial feeling of discomfort, we can experience growth. As you continue to make attempts to communicate more clearly, I encourage you to lean into that discomfort—in other words, allow yourself to be uncomfortable and be curious about it. You will most likely find that growth occurs and clear communication becomes easier.

CHAPTER SIX

Asking for What You Want

In this chapter, we will be working through how to make requests so you can get your needs met in your relationship. This is the fourth and final part of NVC, so let's get to it.

KIM AND AISHA

Kim and Aisha, both in their thirties, have been together for eight years. They each had a previous partner who'd been unfaithful, and it's this similarity that drew them together. Each woman brought a child into the relationship, and the women had agreed to each parent her own child rather than meld the families. This approach worked for many years, but now the kids are in their teens, and the couple is currently struggling with parenting issues.

Kim's son, Jordan, in particular isn't performing well in school. He's not doing his homework and sometimes comes home past his curfew. Kim is stressed by Jordan's behavior. In an attempt to be helpful, Aisha tries to discipline Jordan and enforce consequences. But every time Aisha steps in, Kim feels anxious and protective. To compensate for the guilt she still carries around regarding Jordan's father's behavior, she snaps at Aisha to stop reprimanding Jordan. At first, Aisha was confused by Kim's behavior, but, over time, her confusion has turned to anger.

The issue regarding Jordan's discipline has led to many arguments for a year or so, and the women are at a standstill. During the latest incident, Kim shouted at Aisha in front of Jordan, "Don't talk to my son like that! You have no right to, and you need to stop!" Feeling resentful and irritated, Aisha threw up her hands and left the room in a huff, complaining bitterly under her breath.

Over the course of many weekly sessions, we explored the issues and I explained the process of using NVC skills. During one of the sessions, it emerged that Kim and Jordan had been abused by Kim's previous partner, and Kim had vowed to never let that happen again; she would protect her son at all costs.

When Kim heard Aisha reprimanding her son, it made her feel uneasy and vulnerable, like she wasn't doing her job as a parent or keeping her vow. Although Kim knew Aisha wasn't abusive like her ex, she still felt undermined by her. She needed to protect her son, and she also wanted to be the one to discipline him. But her desire wasn't enough to make that happen. She needed to make a request of her partner to ease up on Jordan and let her take on the role of disciplinarian when the situation called for it.

After we worked through the first three steps (observation, feelings, and needs), I asked Kim what request she wanted to make of Aisha. She immediately said, "Aisha, I don't want you to discipline my son." I stopped her and explained that requests are about what we *want*—not what we *don't want*.

She rephrased her statement: "When I see Jordan getting reprimanded by you, I feel protective. I know I have a need to protect him, and when I can't, I feel anxious. Would you be willing to talk with me first regarding issues related to Jordan's behavior so that I can address them with him?"

When the question was put this way, Aisha's response was much more positive than when Kim simply demanded that Aisha mind her own business. Aisha agreed to speak with Kim when something came up.

Keep in mind that requests may not always be met with a yes, but at least they are being communicated in a productive way.

MAKING THE REQUEST

We usually know quite well what we want from our partner. A big problem is that we usually aren't equipped to ask for what we want in way that is productive and useful. We make demands rather than requests. You can easily recognize demands by how they start. They often sound like this: "You need to . . . ," "Why don't you . . . ," and "You should . . ." There usually aren't any options when you phrase something this way.

On the other hand, a request offers a yes-or-no option. There's no aggression in the request and therefore the person you are making the request of doesn't have to put their figurative fists up. People generally don't want to do what is demanded of them, but when a request is made in a clear and concise way, they are more willing to consider it. Stating a need this way can be refreshing.

Keep It Clear

For several years of their relationship, Kim and Aisha had been willing to tolerate Kim's passive communication style around big issues, but now that the issue involved Jordan's discipline, it was causing arguments and resentment. Kim needed to take a risk and directly ask for what she needed from Aisha. The request she made was clear and to the point: "Would you be willing to talk with me first regarding issues related to Jordan's behavior so that I can address them with him?" When Kim stated it this way, Aisha had the chance to respond either yes or no.

Stay Calm

Keeping emotions in check when asking for what we need is hard, but it is key. The women knew that their emotions would rise when the topic of Jordan's behavior came up, and if Aisha disciplined Jordan, Kim would feel anxious and an argument would ensue. Kim learned not to react to her emotions of the moment and would attempt to maintain a neutral, nonjudgmental stance. She learned to speak calmly to Aisha by focusing on what she needed with regard to disciplining Jordan, which allowed for better communication between the partners.

Use Positive Language

Before they began the work, when Kim and Aisha had discussions around big topics such as Jordan's behavior, they often used sarcastic tones and negative facial expressions, such as rolling their eyes at each other. I encouraged them to table that type of negative behavior and keep their requests of each other positive or at least neutral. This allowed them to listen better to themselves and to each other rather than react to the passive negativity communicated by things like sarcasm and eye rolling.

Be Reasonable

A request is reasonable. It is something the other person is actually able to do if they agree. Unreasonable demands result in defensiveness and disagreement. In the heat of the moment, Kim would bite out, "You need to stay away from my son." And Aisha would shout back, "Don't ever tell me what to do!" Neither of these demands was reasonable. However, once the couple was able to talk about their needs and feelings, they understood better how to keep their requests focused on what the other person could reasonably do to help them meet their needs. When Kim freely expressed her request of Aisha, the tension in the house eased.

MAKE REQUESTS ACTIONABLE

At first blush, telling your partner what you want sounds simple enough, but you need to be careful or your request can border on demanding. Be sure that you don't go overboard with what you are asking and that your request is based in reality. The request Kim made of Aisha to speak to her first with regard to Jordan was well within Aisha's ability to carry out. Making this initial request opened the door for Aisha to make a request of Kim that she, too, could perform if she agreed. With the ability to do what the other asked, their ability to cooperate increased.

Don't Go Overboard

Oftentimes, it can be easy to ask your partner for many things, big and small, when you first learn to make request attempts. It feels good to communicate this way, so you want to keep going. However, if you ask for too many things at once, it can get overwhelming for your partner to try to do them all—and vice versa. Start with something small so you can enjoy some small successes. Making smaller requests and not making too many of them at once will get you into the habit of making—and hearing—bigger requests when they need to be made.

Based in Reality

Many times, Kim and Aisha would discuss one issue, but it would lead into several other unresolved issues. The emotions of the moment would take over and neither partner would be able to think clearly, which would then lead to vague or unreasonable demands that had no basis in reality and were simply not attainable. They learned that in order for their new way of communicating to work, they needed to focus on the facts pertaining to the present issue in order to formulate a realistic request to fulfill the need at hand. The request had to be based in the present and pertain to the issue they were trying to resolve.

NO CONDITIONS ALLOWED

When you make a request, you are simply making a request; you're not attaching any conditions to it. If you do attach a condition, it becomes a demand. Conditional demands often sound something like "If you do this for me, then I will do that for you." Although this statement might sound like compromise, it's still a demand.

For instance, when Kim and Aisha initially agreed that they wouldn't parent each other's kids, the suggestion from Kim sounded like this: "Don't try to parent my child, and I won't try to parent your child." Years later, when Aisha stepped in, presumably to help Kim out with the stress Jordan's behavior was causing, the conditional arrangement they'd made backfired. Conditions only set up couples for failure, disappointment, and resentment.

Fuels Failure

Although the initial conditional demand to parent their own children had good intent, for Kim it came from a place of protection that was not recognized by her or communicated to Aisha. The problem is that when we make demands and attach conditions to them, there's no room to alter them if circumstances change. Kim did need to parent Aisha's daughter from time to time when Aisha wasn't around. This gave Aisha the idea that she, too, could parent Jordan.

In the present situation, Kim was finally able to clearly express her need around the issue of parenting Jordan, and they came to a resolution. Notice that when Kim made her request, she did not include any conditions or promises about her own behavior. In turn Aisha did not agree to the request only if Kim would agree to a request she had. Doing so would have complicated the issue further and made it more likely that one or both would fail to meet the other's demand.

Delivers Disappointment

Demanding things of your partner and promising you'll give in to one of their demands as a compromise may work occasionally. But it usually doesn't work on a consistent basis, which results in one or both partners being disappointed. Because of their history, Kim and Aisha expected each other not to follow through even if they agreed to a request using their new NVC skills. They were used to being disappointed because one or both of them had in the past failed to carry out the other person's demand.

Creates Resentment

Kim and Aisha recognized that years of conditional demands had created resentment between them because one or both of them would fail to meet the condition set forth by the other. Resentment kills emotional intimacy, and years of resentment won't simply go away because you are practicing NVC. The feeling will dissipate, but, depending on the person, the process will be slow, quick, or somewhere in between. Kim and Aisha worked hard through the steps of NVC to slowly chip away at the built-up resentment. They were more willing to meet the requests being made of them, and resentment was slowly replaced by contentment.

Exercise: Recognize Demands and Reframe

Even if you don't have children or the particular issue Kim and Aisha were struggling with, you might still recognize some of their dynamic in your own relationship. Jot down some key points related to their argument, and now think about your own arguments. What demands have you made of each other? Write these down in your notebook. Think about how you might phrase your needs as requests instead.

SAMPLE SCRIPT

Kim hears a heated conversation between Aisha and Jordan through the kitchen window while she is outside working in the yard. She'd just had a conversation with Jordan earlier about his attitude. She puts down the clippers and heads inside. Aisha is reprimanding Jordan about the dirty dishes he'd left in his room, and Jordan is being belligerent.

In the past, Kim would have immediately inserted herself between Aisha and Jordan and demanded that Aisha let her deal with Jordan on her own. This time, Kim uses the NVC skills she's been learning in our sessions.

Kim: *(to herself)* "What am I feeling? . . . I feel angry."

Kim knows she needs to go deeper, and she recognizes that she feels fear that comes from a need to protect Jordan. She also fears that she isn't doing enough to be a good mother to him. But she does not snap at Aisha.

Kim: "Aisha, I see the pile of dirty dishes on the counter that were in Jordan's room. I know that leaving dirty dishes around is not abiding by house rules and that this frustrates you. I get frustrated as well. Would you be willing to let me take over from here? I'll discuss this issue with Jordan."

Because the women have been working on their NVC skills, Aisha recognizes that Kim has identified her feelings and needs and that she is making a request. As the parents in the house, they keep the focus on each other rather than on Jordan. Because Jordan is present, Aisha is mindful to make sure she responds clearly to Kim's request.

Aisha: "Yes, that would be fine. I'll go straighten the living room and come back to the kitchen when you're done."

Aisha appreciated that Kim did not accuse her of interfering and did not demand that she immediately leave the kitchen, which would have resulted in a heated argument in front of Jordan. Aisha exits the room and leaves the parenting of Jordan up to Kim. Jordan remains silent and listens intently to how the adults are communicating.

NVC requests are not demands. They are made with knowledge of one's feelings and one's responsibility for them.

YOUR REQUEST

There's no doubt you have feelings and needs related to an issue about which you and your partner have been at odds. Think about that issue; it could be a recent one or a long-term one. If you've been using your notebook, you've been keeping track of your progress. Now it's time to take the final step in this process and make your request.

PREPARE

What is the action you have been demanding of your partner? How can you turn that demand into a request? Take a moment now to write down a request you can make of your partner. Make sure it is reasonable and doable and has no conditions attached. This is important: If you don't carefully think about your request, it could come across as a demand and fail, and you will continue to be frustrated.

PRACTICE

Have you decided what you want to request? Remember, your request needs to be reasonable and connect back to you. As I mentioned earlier, demands often begin with "You need to . . ." or "Why don't you . . ." or "You should . . ."

Think about how a statement like this might end and then you can usually reverse engineer the statement to determine what your needs and feelings are. For example, you and your partner argue about the upcoming holiday. Your partner wants to spend it with their family again, and you want a small celebration at home. "You should focus on just us for a change!" you shout as the argument concludes without resolution.

Later, when the argument is over and you check in with yourself, you determine that you feel sad. Make a guess about why you feel sad. What unmet need is that feeling centered on? Perhaps you have a need for more intimacy in your relationship. There could be any number of reasons, but try to zero in on what's driving you.

REQUEST EXAMPLE

So you're ready to make your request. As you approach your partner, you may start off with something along the lines of "I'm sad that we don't spend more time creating our own traditions around the holidays. I wonder if you would be willing to celebrate this holiday in a more intimate setting this year."

It may help to imagine approaching your partner with open hands as you make your request. Making a request by starting with "Would you be willing to . . ." or "I wonder if it would be possible . . ." allows your partner to say yes or no without feeling accused or blamed for something.

REFLECT

Does it feel strange to make a request of your partner? If you were not given the ability to make requests in your family when you were growing up, perhaps you feel powerless when it comes to asking for what you want. Or perhaps you've gotten used to the forcefulness of demands. The more often you make a request, the easier and more natural it will become.

CHAPTER SEVEN

Looking Ahead

Thank you for taking the risk to plunge into this book. You could have chosen any book you wanted with the limited time you had, and you chose mine. I appreciate that. I hope you and your partner have come away with some new ideas on how to communicate with each other.

Over the nearly two decades that I've been working with couples and families to help them repair the broken lines of communication, I've found that the more people know themselves, the better they can communicate with those they love. That is the power of NVC.

Objectively looking at a situation, identifying feelings and needs, and making requests are powerful tools that help people process their issues more effectively. These tools have worked not only in my own relationship but also in the relationships of the people who come to me for help. This book includes just a few examples of how NVC worked to help couples resolve their issues, but there are numerous other stories of couples successfully learning to communicate in a more caring, loving, and effective way.

Communication is something we all do every day with any number of people in any number of settings. However, when it comes to our long-term partners, we may find ourselves arguing more often than not. As you've learned, a habit of effective communication as a couple involves four steps: observing the situation, identifying your feelings, stating your needs, and making a request. These steps won't become second nature without consistent practice. Like the couples described in this book, you'll need to work at them and put in the effort together. Let's review them once more.

OBSERVATION

Your first step in NVC is to pay attention to the facts. You've learned the importance of leaving evaluations, judgments, and accusations out of your data-mining mission. You don't make assumptions. You zero in on the circumstances that lead to fights in your relationship. Instead of yelling about everything and anything, you simply acknowledge what is going on in the moment or what went on during the argument.

YOUR FEELINGS

Your second step in NVC is to determine what is going on internally and identify your feelings. Emotions in the moment, which have a tendency to change, are usually at the center of failed communication. Often, we blindly plunge into communicating about a big issue without really understanding what's going on internally. We hurt our partner, and they in turn hurt us because they, too, are acting from an emotional place. Now you are able to talk through a situation and determine what your feelings are at your core. You take responsibility for your feelings with "I" statements. The sooner you decide to figure out what the unknown is, the sooner you can get to solving your communication challenges.

YOUR NEEDS

Your third step in NVC is to figure out what your needs are. Needs are the things that drive you. Remember, everyone has needs. As you and your partner read about and practiced identifying what you each need from your relationship with regard to certain issues, perhaps you've identified both similar needs and opposing needs. Often, when opposing needs meet, arguments and misunderstandings occur, but using your NVC skills, you can voice them to each other and find a way for both of you to get your needs met in a way that works for you as a couple. Knowing your needs and the associated feelings is the start to a relationship where disagreements don't turn into hurtful fights.

REQUESTS

Your fourth step in NVC is to make a request of your partner to get your needs met. When you observe a situation and know what you are feeling and what your unmet needs are, you can ask your partner whether they would be willing to do something specific that will help you meet that need. As you know, there's a very clear distinction between making a demand and making a request. Demands tend to keep us stuck in a cycle of arguments over the same thing again and again. They often put us on the defensive, making it less likely that we will give in to them. On the other hand, requests are kind, considerate, and, most important, focused on your internal needs and feelings—not on what you think your partner can or can't give you.

YOUR NEW APPROACH

As you come to the end of this book, you have essentially learned a new way of communicating in your relationship. If you start using the NVC steps with your partner, you will most assuredly have a very different experience in your relationship going forward. What's more, if you have children in your home, they will notice that this new style of communication is creating a less argumentative atmosphere, and you will likely start communicating with them differently as well. The change may be small at first, but the more consistent you are, the more your NVC skills will become habitual.

This long-term relationship you are in is one that is worth keeping. You've had many good times and positive experiences as a couple. You've probably just fallen into a rut, which has affected how you communicate. But now you know that there is another way, a way that can restart your long-term relationship. You can take a new path.

We aren't given many opportunities to change things in life, but this is one of those rare circumstances where you do have a choice to do things differently. Are you going to make it? This book has given you the knowledge and the tools. It's given you the inside scoop on how to take your relationship down a path of effective communication. It's now up to you to determine whether you want to use the knowledge and skills. If you dare to be courageous and do things differently, you won't regret it.

References

Fisher, Helen. "Lust, Attraction, Attachment: Biology and Evolution of the Three Primary Emotion Systems for Mating, Reproduction, and Parenting." *Journal of Sex Education and Therapy* 25, no. 1 (2000):96–104. doi.org /10.1080/01614576.2000.11074334.

Gottman, John. *Why Marriages Succeed or Fail: And How You Can Make Yours Last.* New York, NY: Simon & Schuster, 1995.

Lamidi, Esther, and Wendy D. Manning. "Marriage and Cohabitation Experiences Among Young Adults." National Center for Family & Marriage Research. Accessed May 1, 2019. www.bgsu.edu/ncfmr/resources/data /family-profiles/lamidi-manning-marriage-cohabitation-young-adults -fp-16-17.html.

Index

Acknowledgments

When I started as an 18-year-old in college I never thought that someday I would be helping people in their relationships. A lot of my understanding of couple dynamics initially came from education. The practical application of it, though, has come from my wife. She is truly my better half. My life is better because of her, and my children are great humans because of her.

About the Author

Dr. David Simonsen has been in practice for 19 years as a licensed marriage and family therapist. During that time he has helped hundreds of families and couples work through issues causing problems in their relationships. He is a husband, father, son, and brother. He loves Disneyland and traveling around in an RV. You can find out more about him at DocDavid.net.